Praise for the Poetry of Jack

Author of Over Twenty #1 Best Sellers / Hund₁

CW00862790

— Bukowski's Ghos‗

Winner: Best Poetry Collection of 2016 (eFestival of Words)

"With *Bukowski's Ghost*, Jackson Dean Chase invokes the spirit of the greatest poet of our time with the respect and admiration he deserves. This is an honest, intense, and remarkable collection by **a fresh and powerful new voice**."
—Terry Trueman, Printz Honor author of *Stuck in Neutral*

"Poems immersed in **the despair of the lost, broken, and lonely**."
—Kindle reviewer (UK)

— Love at the Bottom of the Litter Box —

"If you love cats, if you've ever struggled to make it, then **you will love this book**."
—Kindle reviewer

— Christmas Eve in the Drunk Tank —

"A crazy collection of weird winter and holiday-themed poems **sure to bring a twisted smile to the face of Charles Bukowski fans**."
—Kindle reviewer

— Be the Magic —

"...**This book will help in a real, deep, and lasting way**."
—Kindle reviewer

— Death of a Scratching Post —

"What really caught me about this collection was the **raw emotion** and the no-holds-barred way of looking at life. **It's the best kind of poetry there is**—with a subtle and rhythmic flow to the writing and **strong emotional messages**, delivered both bluntly and through **delightful** cat metaphors."
—The Underground

— Worms Ate Your Face —

"A sense of **supernatural dread** runs through it like an untapped vein..."
—Kindle reviewer

BOOKS BY JACKSON DEAN CHASE

Fiction
Beyond the Dome series:
#0 Hard Times in Dronetown
#1 Drone: A Young Adult Dystopian Thriller
#2 Warrior (coming soon)

Stand Alone Horror Novels
Wish for Death: A Novel of Genie Horror & Possession (coming soon)

Young Adult Horror series:
#1 Come to the Cemetery
#2 The Werewolf Wants Me
#3 The Haunting of Hex House
#4 Gore Girls: Twisted Tales & Poems
#5 Lost Girls: Twisted Tales & Poems
#6 Horror Girls: Twisted Tales & Poems
#7 Killer Young Adult Fiction (complete series + extras)

Poetry
Raw Underground Poetry series:
#1 Bukowski's Ghost
#2 Love at the Bottom of the Litter Box
#3 Christmas Eve in the Drunk Tank
#4 Be the Magic
#5 Death of a Scratching Post
#6 Worms Ate Your Face
Best of #1: Crazy Cat Poems for Crazy Cat People

Non-Fiction
Story Secrets for Writers series:
#1 How to Start Your Novel
#2 How to Start Your Novel Workbook

How to Write Realistic Fiction series:
#1 How to Write Realistic Characters
#2 How to Write Realistic Men
#3 How to Write Realistic Monsters, Aliens, and Fantasy Creatures

Writers' Phrase Book series:
#1 Horror Writers' Phrase Book
#2 Post-Apocalypse Writers' Phrase Book
#3 Action Writers' Phrase Book
#4 Fantasy Writers' Phrase Book
#5 Fiction Writers' Phrase Book (series sampler)
#6 Science Fiction Writers' Phrase Book
#7 Romance, Emotion, and Erotica Writers' Phrase Book

— BEST of RAW UNDERGROUND POETRY —

CRAZY

CAT POEMS

for CRAZY CAT PEOPLE

(The Complete Bukowski, Cats, and Me)

JACKSON DEAN
CHASE

www.JacksonDeanChase.com

For cat lovers and cat crazies.

Thanks to my editor, C. Graves, for years of heartfelt perseverance shaping my talent. This book would not exist without you.

Special Thanks to Julie Stafford and Tina Simon.

First Printing, November 2016

ISBN-13: 978-1540339911
ISBN-10: 1540339912

Published by Jackson Dean Chase, Inc. / Printed by CreateSpace

PUBLISHER'S NOTE

For **FREE** books and more, visit the author at:

www.JacksonDeanChase.com

— CONTENTS —

Love at the Bottom of the Litter Box

Death of a Scratching Post

Paws and Claws: New Scratchings

— INTRODUCTION —

"There's a fine line between
being crazy about cats
and just plain crazy."

Cats make everything better. You're here, so you must feel the same. You love the way your cats look at you, the way they curl up in your lap. The purrs, the paws, that wise twitch of the tail. You'll do anything for your cats. They're part of you. Now imagine you're part of them . . .

Welcome to *Crazy Cat Poems for Crazy Cat People*. This book collects all my best selling poems about cats from *Love at the Bottom of the Litter Box* and *Death of a Scratching Post*, plus *Paws and Claws: New Scratchings*, ten poems I've prepared exclusively for this special edition.

These poems explore the joy of living with cats, the pain of losing them, and the challenge to be a cat surrounded by dogs. It's not just about being a cat person, it's about being alone, about struggling to create art in a mad world, a world that doesn't understand and doesn't want to.

If you've ever struggled to express yourself, to be your authentic true self, this book knows how you feel. It's sad, funny, and thoughtful.

This book is you, for you, by you and people like you. *Crazy cat people yearning to be free.*

Jackson Dean Chase

www.JacksonDeanChase.com

P.S.: If you enjoy this book, please post a review. Thanks!

THE BUKOWSKI CONNECTION

I'll be honest: I never thought much of poetry. I was forced to write my first poem for tenth-grade English. It was about a vampire rising from her coffin and my teacher called it "garbage" while teaching what I thought was the most boring, pretentious nonsense ever. So I tuned out. The only poetry I enjoyed from then on were song lyrics, which I didn't think of as poetry at all.

It wasn't until years later that I discovered Charles Bukowski—first through his crazy stories, then his poems. Finally, here was a poet I could appreciate! He talked about real things, real hurts, and he was funny and sad and strangely invincible to himself and his critics.

Bukowski was not bound by strict rules, but by emotion. His poetry came from the heart and the gut, the rawness seeping out of him like bile. No topic was taboo, no truth hidden. Poetry was finally torn down from the ivory towers and given back to the people. This was Bukowski's magic, his gift to the world, and it had such a profound effect on me that I had no choice but to create my own.

While I write all kinds of poetry from the inspirational to the tragic, those collected here are about me, my cats, and my life as a poet and as a man—*the personal made public*. They are from a time in my life when I was grasping for love, for wisdom and success—sometimes finding them, sometimes not.

Like Bukowski, my life is made of highs and lows, humor and despair. It's not always a pretty picture, but it is an honest one.

Note: Read more poems about and inspired by the mad genius of Charles Bukowski in my award-winning poetry collection, *Bukowski's Ghost: Poems for Old Souls in New Bodies*. Check out the preview on page 88.

LOVE

at the BOTTOM of the LITTER BOX

(Bukowski, Cats, and Me: Volume 1)

Cats vs. Humans

The cat does what it wants:
    sleeping,
    playing,
    hunting,
    feeding.
Occasionally, it mates.
There is nobility in its simplicity,
a nobility we humans lack.
Despite all our science and religion,
our social constructs fail
to make up for what we have lost:
    that connection to the earth,
    to our elemental selves—
        wild,
            animal,
                free.

WITH CATS

Love does not come easy
    except with cats.
With cats, there is everything to love
and nothing that cannot be forgiven.

No Animal

Dogs are dirty,
cats are clean.
But people?
We're clean on the outside
and dirty within.
We pretend to love,
to be loyal
in ways no animal ever could.

CAT PEOPLE

If only people were like cats,
    I might understand them.
        Hell, I might even like them!

You Had Me at "Meow"

You had me at "meow," my friend.
You had me with three sleepy blinks,
with the tender flick of your tail,
the purr in your throat.
You had me with all these things:
treasured moments
curling in my lap.

It Still Hurts

I knew her less than two years,
but she was the greatest friend I ever had,
better than all the people I've known.
Her friendship and loyalty were without equal,
without complication.

She was always there,
until she wasn't.

Her death left a hole in me
that can never be filled.
I try to explain,
but others cannot understand
the depth of our love
or the majesty of that cat's soul.

PURE LOVE FROM PURE SOULS

I live with two beautiful cats, Ginger and Mary Ann.
I named them after *Gilligan's Island*.
Their personalities match
the characters from the show:
    Ginger is aloof and demanding,
      a movie star.
    Mary Ann is friendly and cheerful,
      the girl next door.
They are my constant companions, nurturing me
with pure love from pure souls.
My cats are better friends to me
than I have been to others:
    more accepting,
    more playful,
    more loving.
I realized this tonight
and wept.

Love at the Bottom of the Litter Box

A friend called, told me she had a litter of kittens.
Did I want one?
I said, "Hell yes! Gimme the best you got."
The kitten had every damn spot and stripe
you could want on a cat.
She could talk—
    not in words, but in meaning.
Her meow was an old telephone ring dialing my heart.
But she had fleas and three kinds of worms
pouring out her ass like string-cheese.
She shit everywhere:
Diarrhea all over my walls,
carpet ruined.
I took her to the vet,
spent a month's rent trying to fix her:
    Fleas dead,
    worms gone,
    and she *still* had diarrhea!
I thought about getting rid of her,
but she loved me too much,
and that's the one thing
I can't say no to.

THEY'D RATHER SUFFER

I hear the scratching in the litter box,
my cat straining to go,
then more scratching to cover what came out.
I sigh, hoping she pooped all right.
This cat's got problems.
She's on a special diet that helps,
but sooner or later, it's diarrhea time.
An hour passes, maybe more.
I haven't seen the cat,
so I go looking.
I find her,
lift her tail.
To my horror,
a cement-like raft of shit is
glued to her hind leg.
I grab the scissors to cut it off.
"Here kitty," I say. "Nice kitty! Hold still for Daddy . . ."
As soon as I get close,
she runs,
which is what happens
whenever I try to help anyone.

WORTHLESS

Last night, my cat kept trying to climb my bookshelf,
claws sinking into spines,
shredding pages.
I'd been trying to sleep
and her bullshit wasn't helping.
I growled and hissed,
squirting her with water,
chasing her around the house screaming,
    "I'll kill you! You used to be good,
    but now you're worthless.
    Nobody loves you.
    No one will miss you when you're gone!"
The cat stared at me
with big, scared eyes.
I realized then
I wasn't talking to her at all:

I was talking to myself.

HALLOWEEN IN HELL

Black cats and witches,
greedy children with grasping hands,
stay away from my door.
   Little bastards!
You'll get no tricks, no treats,
   not from me.
I have my lights off for a reason:
   broken heart in one hand,
   bottle in the other.
Leave me to my torment,
   it will be yours soon enough . . .

FRIENDS

When I was a child,
books were my only friends.
Now, I have cats.
I keep trying to add people,
but it never works.
It always ends the same,
with me lying face down,
   shattered
in a pool of misplaced trust.

CHESHIRE CAT

From across the room, I see you:
   too beautiful for words.
Smiling, I back away
and feel myself fade:
   invisible,
     safe,
       alone.

TODAY

Today is the day when love lies dreaming
    as Mexicans cut my grass,
    as cats yowl and dogs bark,
    as the phone rings and bills mount,
    as my parents inch toward their graves,
    and I speed toward mine,
    somewhere, a girl thinks of me
    and I, of her.
We shared something once,
a moment of passion.
Now we share this memory
and wonder what might have been . . .

IT'S CLOSE

I never understood my ex-girlfriend.
Just when I thought I did,
she would do something
   alien,
     emotional,
something that would push me away
instead of bringing us together.
I miss the small, quiet moments with her
more than the sex,
and certainly more than the fights.
Maybe I'm better off alone.
It's easier, and I have my cats.
But as much love as they give,
it's not the same.
   It can't be,
     but it's close.

ONLY MY CATS REMAIN

I've always been shy around women.
That's why I never picked you:
    I let you pick me.
And I tried to be the man you wanted,
But you left me, like everyone does.
Only my cats remain—
    aloof,
        mysterious,
            like me.

MOVING DAY

As the cat purrs in my lap,
    as Mozart pours from my speakers,
I drink this wine
    and write these words,
    feeling the first relief I've known in days.
The heaviness leaves me,
    the hurt you caused becoming less
    as you move from my present into my past,
    never to return.

THE WOMAN THING

Things have been bothering me lately—
not a lot, but enough.
There's always the money thing,
the career thing,
but worst of all is the woman thing.
That's what's eating me now:
  the memory of you.
In my house, I can't forget.
So I put on my leather jacket
and pull my baseball cap low,
stepping into cold November rain.
I take a long walk to clear my head.
I don't look at the people smoking on doorsteps
    or hurrying past.
This isn't about meeting anyone
    (that's the last thing I need).
I just want to be alone with myself:
    no bills,
    no internet,
    no women,
just me and the night.

It's quiet out. Peaceful.
The rain isn't bad, and I even manage to whistle a tune—
    not too cheerful, but it's a start.
I walk to the library,

drawing inspiration from the shelves.
I check out some books by Bukowski,
and a DVD of his poetry readings.

When I get home, I feel better.
The cats greet me at the door,
an onslaught of head-bonks to show their love.
I check my messages, relieved you haven't called
    (no one has).
I pop Buk's DVD into the computer.
The old man appears on the screen,
drunk and rowdy as ever.
The audience loves Buk as much he hates them,
and maybe that's a metaphor for our relationship:
    Love, hate.
        Hate, love.
    Both of us sick with separate needs—
        you, desperate to get in,
            me, desperate to get out.
But I want to forget all that, so I return to the show.
It's a beautiful riot, the old man vs. the mob.
    They're evenly matched
    as the wine flows
    and the words come.

    Point the way, Buk.
        Point the way!

Halfway through, he does.

Inspiration hits, or maybe it's the wine.
I write a poem, a damn good one—
    one I can hear Buk narrating in my mind.
And when it's done, I write another,
and another . . .

The best time to write is when
the pain's still fresh,
the hurt's too deep.

It makes me glad the women leave
because I get to keep these poems instead.

WHAT LIFE IS

I don't know why I want to be a poet.
It just seems terribly important now,
despite hating poems my whole life.
The only poet I really like
    (the only one I can stand)
is Charles Bukowski.
That sad old man,
the vulgar man with the alcoholic soul.
He's the one who makes the words look easy
because sometimes he's not very good.
He talks too much about racetracks
and all the shitty people in his life,
but most of all, he talks about the beer.

I don't gamble and I don't drink
(well, not too much),
and I don't let shitty people into my life—
at least not after that last bunch of assholes.
In fact, I hardly let anyone in at all
    except my cats,
and sometimes, even they feel like too much,
but they're better than having no one at all.

I spend all day hunched over my computer
wanting to write half as good as Bukowski.
Bukowski at his best,

when he wasn't drunk or not drunk enough
to write about his boring day
instead of his interesting life.

I write until my brain hurts and fingers bleed,
a red smear of truth from the bucket of my soul.

Now it's late, past midnight.
I have to piss.
I go to the bathroom,
   trip over the cats,
   hit the light,
   and whip out my dick.
I pick up that new book of Bukowski poems,
one of five hundred released after he died.
I open it to the page I've bookmarked,
hoping for a chuckle
or some kind of inspiration,
but it's another one about beer.

The worst part is
I think my dick's aiming into the toilet,
but it's really pointed at the floor.

NINE MINUTES

It's 11:51 pm.
I have nine minutes to write this poem.
   OK, now eight . . .

This is a pressure test
to prove I can write sixteen poems today.
   Seven minutes left . . .

The other poems came so fast, so easy
it doesn't seem fair.
But I'm going to do it
even if it kills me.
Even if it kills YOU.
   Six minutes on the clock . . .

Countdown to the end.
Brain racing, grasping at straws.
Say something prophetic, profound,
or just amuse the dumb apes.
Who cares?
   Five minutes . . .

Fuck! Where did the time go?
The minutes slipping by
like the days of my life.
Going, going, gone!

No idea how to get them back.
    Four . . .

And maybe that's the point:
there is no return ticket,
no way to recapture the magic of the past.
There is only the pain of now,
the promise of tomorrow.
    Three . . .

I'm still thinking of what to say,
what to do.
Not just with this poem, but my life.
    Two . . .

This is it, the end is near!
Feel the blood racing,
thoughts pumping,
frantic, going nowhere.
And yet I keep trying,
keep clawing.
I can't give up.
    One . . .

Nothing genius comes to mind.
No wisdom, not even a chuckle.
I know it's over.
I wait,
resigned, relieved

as the clock ticks and the cat yawns,
oblivious to my suffering.
Midnight!

Time's up, I passed.
One poem in nine minutes . . .

Congratulations, me.

WORKAHOLIC

People tell me to get some rest,
concerned I do not sleep but toil,
ceaseless and alone.
They cannot believe how much I do:
   300 poems in 60 days.
It seems impossible to them,
yet normal to me.
I sleep just fine,
and I'm not alone:

   I have my cats,
   my words,
   and you.

ALREADY THERE

I'm trying to write this poem,
and the cat won't stop bugging me.
She plows into my bare leg,
head-bonking me
with loud purrs.
I reach down and pet her,
hope she'll go away.
I have to get this poem done,
but she comes back,
pawing my leg.
It feels good until the claws come out.
I curse, but pet her anyway,
write a few more lines.
The cat comes back,
jumping on my desk,
getting in my chair,
but not my lap.
I pet her some more.
She goes away.
I write until I hear a loud noise from across the room.
The cat is knocking shit over on purpose.
"Hey!" I yell. "No!"
We exchange a look.
She stops screwing around.
I go back to writing
and then she is plowing into my leg again,

looking at me with those green, green eyes,
    the eyes that love me more than anyone,
    more than I love myself.
I can't work like this,
not with constant interruptions!
And the cat is pressing her wet nose into my leg
like she's trying to put her love inside me.

> *Doesn't she know*
> *it's already there?*

THE LIFE OF A HERMIT

On any given day,
   I will wake up,
   curse,
   crack my knuckles,
   stare at the ceiling,
   wish for another hour of sleep,
   wish for a whole new life,
   rise and pet the cats,
     tell them they are beautiful,
   then piss,
   and pour myself an energy drink.

I stare at my computer
   expecting today is the day
   I will be discovered
   and everything will change.

I answer emails,
   tweet and retweet things,
   check my blog stats,
   eat a processed meat stick,
   open a document,
   and write poems.

When the time comes, I take a shit,
   reading Bukowski on the toilet,

taking comfort in his words.

I eat a sandwich and watch TV,
    wanting my life to be like a sitcom
    instead of a tragedy.

I write some more poems,
    take another shit
    like a hobbit's second breakfast.
    While I am there,
    I will jot down a few poems by hand
    as I wait for it all to come out
    (the words and the shit).

I go back to the computer,
check my email, my social media.
I'm still not famous, so I curse
    and break things
    until the cats look at me in alarm.

I eat dinner and watch TV, maybe a movie—
    an old one, like my soul.
After the movie is over, I take a shower.
I even get dressed,
though I have nowhere to go.

I stare at myself in the mirror:
    getting older, poorer,
    more desperate,

more loved yet unloved,
more real yet less real.

I clean the cats' litter box
and can't believe how two tiny animals
can fill three boxes so consistently.
I sigh, remembering the cats are my only friends
so I will accept their shit, as they accept mine.

I stare into the night,
at the train tracks and the train on it.
I want to run out of my apartment
and ride the rails like a hobo.
I want the train to take me far from here,
far from this miserable life,
    but I am too tired,
    and it is too late to run—
    from here or anywhere.

I go to sleep and dream,
hoping tomorrow will be different,
    but secretly,
        I know
            it will be
                just
                    the
                        same.

A Good Day

Today is a good day:
    I slept well, ate good.
The sun shone as I played with my cats,
and I even summoned the Muse
to write this poem.
Tomorrow won't be a good day:
    I'll be evicted from my home,
        from this life that broke my heart
            and stomped my soul.
I'll be just another broke, starving poet
wandering mad, alone.
Friendless, cat-less,
with no pen, no paper,
no way to write these words that keep me sane.
But today?

    Today is a good day:
        the last I'll ever have.

ONE LAST POEM

There's an eviction notice on my door,
a breakup text on my phone,
and a stack of unpaid bills
waiting to strangle me.
I have no money,

> no job,

> no love,

> no time.

But I have my words:

> the words of a poet,

> the words of a fool.

Wisdom and madness
that are worth millions
if only I could find:

> the right agent,

> the right publisher,

> the right woman,

> the right friends,

> *people who believe.*

I've never been good at connecting.
Sooner or later, everyone pulls away,
leaving me with

> my emptiness,

> my sorrow,

> my sad, bitter self.

I should never have been born!

This world is too hard, too cruel,
too obsessed with everything
I care nothing about.

My cats watch me pace and moan.
They don't understand
        there will be no more kibble,
        no more clean litter boxes,
        no more me.

There is only this one last poem.

DEATH

of a SCRATCHING POST

(Bukowski, Cats, and Me: Volume 2)

DEATH OF A SCRATCHING POST

Life is a cat:
   capricious,
      sharp of claw,
         but not without a sense of humor.
Like a cat, life is mysterious, inscrutable.
It does what it wants
because it knows no other way:
   giving a playful nip,
      working its claws in,
         drawing blood as it purrs contentedly.
Life treats us as its scratching post,
   a well-loved tool,
      a toy to practice its killing ways.
It leaves us old, tattered, torn,
ready to be replaced
when there is no more fun to be had.
We die as Life twitches its tail and moves on.

MAGNIFICENT BEASTS

There's a cat inside us,
biting, clawing to get out.
    This cat is wild—
    it wants to be free,
    to return to its feral roots.
It doesn't understand jobs, laws, taxes.
It only understands what we have forgotten:
    our connection to nature,
    our desire to roam free and unfettered
    like the magnificent beasts we are.

An Empty Bowl

I wake covered in cat scratches,
to a pair of guilty eyes mourning an empty bowl.
I don't know how I slept through the pain;
I must've really been out of it.
I rub at the wounds, wince, and get up, grumbling.
The cat watches me stagger into the kitchen,
crowds in as I pour kibble into her bowl.
She chews happily,
no longer afraid of starvation.
Me, I open the refrigerator,
staring into empty hell.
Who's going to refill my bowl?
I turn to ask the cat,
but she's already gone.
I guess I'll just stand here and wait
if I don't starve to death first.

A CAT'S LOVE

Sometimes, I wonder how much of a cat's love
comes from needing something:
    food, attention,
    a warm place to sleep,
    a clean box to shit in.
The only other time they come around
is to mark their territory,
rubbing their body against mine
to remind themselves
(and the rest of the world)
that I am theirs.
Then they're off again,
doing cat things in cat places,
living another life in another world.
It's a place I can never be part of,
no matter how hard I try.

    Come to think of it,
        cats are a lot like people.

"MEOW"

Have you ever noticed humans have
a million different words to say the same thing?
Cats have one:
    One meow to say, "I love you,"
    one to say, "I'm sorry,"
    one to say, "Forgive me,"
    and one for, "Thank you."
Cats don't need more than one word for each,
so why do we?
Why do we feel the need
to fill dictionaries and thesauri,
book after book
with more and more complicated ways
to say what we really mean?
What's the point?
It only makes things harder,
    more confusing,
    more lonely.
Cats know this.
That's why they stopped at "Meow."

LIVING WITH CATS

Living with cats is the closest I'll come
    to having children,
    to living with anyone ever again.
This doesn't make me as sad as it would some.
My work is my life;
I don't have a lot to give outside
    these words on the page,
    these screams in my head.
I can't sustain friendships,
let alone relationships.
Hell, I can't even go to parties!
They require too much of me.
People require too much.
But not cats.
Cats are simple!
They want the same things I want
    (aside from a dead bird or two).
That makes it easy.
Cats don't judge,
they don't scold,
they simply are . . .

    The way I wish people were.

CRAZY CAT LADY

I never understood the old woman down the street,
the one with a hundred cats that would come
    prowling and yowling,
    breeding and feeding,
    with enough gold eyes to light up a freeway.
The neighbors and I made fun of her,
called her the "Crazy Cat Lady"
because that's what she was—
    but at least she wasn't alone,
    which was more than I could say for me.

So one day I got myself a cat (just one),
and her whiskers brushed away some of my pain.
Then I got two more,
then ten,
and each time,
they took more of my pain away.
I kept on collecting them,
haunting shelters, scouring Craigslist ads,
leaving bowls of tuna by the back door.
Soon, I had more cats than I knew what to do with:
    cat hair,
    cat shit,
    but most of all,
    cat love.

I never felt so needed, so important,
which is something I never got from people.

Now the neighbors make fun of me,
call me "crazy" too,
but I'll have the last laugh:

How much love do they have?

THE PEACEFUL MINGLING
OF SOFT-FURRED SOULS

I have met many more people than I have cats,
but have always preferred the company of the latter.
I can know cats deeply in an instant—
    there is no awkwardness,
    no holding back,
    only the magic of connection.
The peaceful mingling of soft-furred souls,
souls that expect and desire no more than
    food,
      shelter,
        love,
all the living, giving things
without pretext or complication.
Cats present themselves as they really are,
    as I am,
and wish you could be.

I Love Cats, But . . .

I love cats, but they don't love me,
at least not in the way I want them to.
They won't come when I call;
they simply stare then walk away.
It's always the same,
no matter how much I beg,
no matter how much I need them,
they're never there.
Except sometimes
when they surprise me,
leaping into my lap,
creeping into my bed.
It's affection on their terms,
    not mine,
and I know I should resent it,
but I take it all the same.

FURRY LITTLE ALARM CLOCKS

How can my cats sleep so much
when they won't let me do the same?
I've tried to tell them with words,
with grunts and growls,
by pushing them away.
Yet they keep coming to wake me up,
furry little alarm clocks
with cold noses and heavy paws.
I can only put them off so long
before the claws come out . . .
just a little pressure at first,
then digging in,
scratching me until my eyes open,
bewildered, cursing, getting up,
chasing them away.
I look back at my bed,
knowing I need that extra hour of sleep,
but there's no way I'm going to get it.

The cats have won again.

MUSIC FOR CATS

Sometimes, I sing to my cats,
swapping out the lyrics for "meows."
They don't seem to mind—
   as long as I feed them.

A Pain So Deep

You say you love me,
and I believe you,
but I cannot *feel* it.
This fills me with sorrow,
with a pain so deep, it poisons me.
I've been betrayed enough
I'm suspicious of everyone:
    friends, family, lovers.
I cannot feel the *truth* of their love,
like I cannot feel yours.
I know it sounds crazy, but
love raises too many questions
with too many ways you can hurt me.
At least with cats, I know where I stand.
But with people?
    Never.

Friend for Life

How can I spend one minute with a cat
and know I have a friend for life,
yet there are people I have known for decades
that continue to find new ways to hurt me?
With the cat, there is
    no doubt,
    no fear,
    no wasted tears,
    or boring conversations.
There is no sleeping on the couch
or desperate waiting for the phone to ring.
There are no recriminations,
no justifications.
The cat loves simply,
and expects the same.

    Why do humans have to ruin love
    by complicating everything?

UNDER MIDNIGHT SKIES

I have slunk down alleys
under midnight skies
the only sound the mating of cats.
Each time, I had to get out,
had to be free to think, to move,
to feel the cold wind at my back,
the hard truth in my heart
that though this world is not for me,
    I must be for it.
I must find a way to belong,
to leave something behind
as the cats scream
and the clouds slip over the moon.

AFTER DARK

The cat creeps,
    the clock ticks,
        and I,
            I am alone.

BLACK CAT

My love is a black cat, feral and wild.
　　It slips between shadows,
　　　　hunting impossible prey.

Hoping Against Hope

I opened the refrigerator door
and the cats came tearing in,
hoping against hope there would be tuna,
or wet food,
even lunch meat scraps.
But no, there was only people food,
full of garlic and onions
and all the things I love and cats hate.
You'd think the bastards would have figured it out by now,
but there they go,
twisting around my legs,
mewing for a sniff
and perhaps a taste.
The cats urge me to bring my dinner close,
and when I do,
they turn up their noses
and saunter off,
giving me sideways, offended looks
as if it's my fault we don't eat the same food.
Well, maybe it is.
Maybe if I sold less books and wasn't so famous,
I'd be opening a can of cat food right now . . .
and you can be damn sure I wouldn't be sharing it.

THE CAT WHO SAVED MY LIFE

I'd been feeling down for weeks,
and by down, I mean suicidal.
Even my cat couldn't cheer me up.
She watched me, worried when
frantic paws and plaintive mews
failed to get a response.
Her food was low and her litter box high,
her favorite toy rolled under the couch
   and out of sight
   like my hopes and dreams.
It was all I could do to tell her I was sorry,
that she'd be better off without me.
"There must be good homes somewhere," I told her.
She just stared and flicked her tail.
I climbed into bed with my iPod,
put in my earbuds, and hit "repeat" on
some self-help shit I'd downloaded.
I didn't really think it would work, but at this point,
I was desperate enough to try anything.
The recording told me to relax,
that everything would be all right . . .
I fell asleep and woke to silence
with my earbud wires chewed to pieces,
the goddamn cat grinning
like she'd just saved me from a pair of snakes.

I wanted to be mad,
but she was so proud of herself
it didn't seem right,
so I laughed and thanked her instead.
Who knows?
Maybe she saved my life after all.

COME, FRIENDS!

There is music to be made
and songs to be sung!
Chattering and yowling
at each passing bird,
each swatting paw,
an endless chorus
until our last meow.

NINE LIVES LIVED,
NINE LIVES LOST

I saw my girl squashed by the road,
picked clean by time.
She'd survived countless fleas, ticks, worms,
and even me,
but not this.
The tires of some heartless bastard,
some drunk piece of shit,
had left their hateful mark on
her once-great beauty.
I look down, seeing
   nine lives lived,
   nine lives lost,
never looking back,
never knowing
it would come to this,
gone in the blink of an eye.
I lift my girl up,
a mangled angel,
and bury her in the backyard.
No one sees my tears,
no one knows my pain.
I am her pallbearer,
   priest,
and mourner all in one.

WRITER'S BLOCK

As a poet, I often lose myself in quiet contemplation,
the words and images symbols
for past hurts and present goals.
So many important things to be said,
yet read by so few.
    It's not fair!
People tell me they hate poetry,
but love mine.
I understand because I hate poetry too.
Not all of it, not Bukowski
or the others that matter,
the ones who tell it like it is.
Maybe I'll write a poem about them,
    or one about me,
one that will get people's attention,
make them see poetry isn't just
greeting cards and Shakespeare.
Maybe *this* poem will be my masterpiece,
the one that catapults me to fame and fortune.
I place my fingers on the keys,
anxious to summon the Muse,
but all I get is the cat rubbing up against me,
waiting to be fed,
and the bills mounting up,
waiting to be paid.

I get an ordinary day packed with the bullshit of life,
of a world that grinds us down,
that leaves no time for art,
no time to create,
no time for anything
but to be a cog in the machine.
Eat, sleep, shit,
and earn enough money to keep doing it
until you roll over into your grave
to make room for the next generation.
The idiots don't understand
    there is more to life than living,
the same way they don't understand anything
except football, beer, and knuckling under
to false truths and broken promises.
They couldn't write a poem if they tried,
not even if you gave them all the time in the world.
When the words won't come,
I almost feel like I'm one of them, but worse,
because I know the difference.
I know I can be something more,
    something bigger,
    something *great!*
Impatient claws find my leg,
working their way toward my knee.
Another distraction . . .
I get up, feed the cat,
then sit at my computer and wait.

CONVERSATION WITH A CAT

I'm figuring out the puzzle on the back of a cereal box
when the cat walks in and demands my attention.
    "Meow," she says.
"Meow," I reply. "What's up?"
    Not much. I came to remind you I'm still here.
"That's nice," I tell her then look back at the puzzle.
Goddamn Lucky Charms!
I found the blue moon,
but where's the purple horseshoe?
    "Meow," the cats says again.
"What is it?"
    I noticed you weren't paying attention to me.
"I'm busy."
    That's because you're doing the wrong thing again.
"Like what?"
    Like looking at things that don't matter.
    Listen, there's a bird outside!
"So?"
    So, we should go get it. It'll be fun.
"I'm having fun where I am."
    No, you're not. You're just sitting there!
    You're always sitting there.
    I've sat in your chair
    and looked at the same things,
    at the cereal box,
    at the computer,

the TV,
at a hundred different things you find interesting
and I've come to a conclusion.
"What's that?" I asked.
You're an idiot.
Before I can answer, the bird lands outside my window.
I put the Lucky Charms down
and follow the cat to the glass
wondering what she sees
that I don't.

CATS KNOW

There are things cats know that people don't.
Like how to live,
how to love,
how to simply be
    yourself
as nature intended.
The cats stare at us,
disbelieving our choices
the crazy things we do,
how we choose
    work over sleep,
    work over play,
    work over love,
    work over everything.
Cats know better because they are better.
They don't clutter their lives
with needless complications.
They are here to enjoy themselves,
and unlike people,
they leave nothing behind but their love.

PAWS &

CLAWS

NEW SCRATCHINGS

(Bukowski, Cats, and Me: Volume 3)

I Am Not That Man

I am old, older than I look,
but younger than I feel.
I spend most of my time alone
with two cats and two lives:
one for the public,
and one for me.
I keep a few friends but no lovers,
and this makes me an exception
to be pitied,
to be constantly told that someday,
      if I am lucky,
I will find the right woman
and my life will change:
the grump, the curmudgeon, the hermit,
all will be swept away,
replaced by some pleasant,
soft-spoken man who buys his wife flowers.
But I am not that man,
and while I hold certain romantic ideals,
I do not do well with romance.
I do not pursue it,
do not desire to pursue it.
Real love is messy;
I prefer my relationships to be on the page,
as easy to quit as to begin,
and always a comfort.

TRAPPED IN A WORLD OF DOGS

I've felt like a cat my whole life:
    a cat trapped in a world of dogs.
This poem is for people like me
    and people like you.
It is for those who love cats more than humans.
Those who struggle to exist,
    who live on the fringe.
Those for whom the outside world means little
because it offers none of the love and security of cats,
nor their quiet, simple acceptance.
    Cats are a warm, furry barrier
    against this cold, cruel world.
    Sometimes, that's enough . . .
    Sometimes.

SCRATCHING AT
THE WINDOW OF LIFE

My feline soul scratches
at the window of life,
dying to get out,
dying to stay in.
In, where it's safe.
In, where it's warm;
where I have a full belly
and empty heart.
Outside, the enemy dwells,
hot heads and cold logic,
a world of handshakes,
a world of smiles
that hide sharp teeth.
Outside, I have no control.
Instead, I have fear,
that terrible, tingling fascination of
    "What if?"
    What if I got out?
    What if I got past this glass wall I've built?

MY BEST FRIENDS ARE CATS

My best friends are cats.
They are me, and I am them.
We both love our routines
and hate anything that disturbs them.
We do what we want,
when we want.
We're happy being alone,
but happy to be together when it suits us.
We're loyal.
We love deeply,
and when that love is broken,
we slink away to lick our wounds.
We'll never fit in,
even when we try.
Especially when we try.
And so we stop trying to fit in
and start trying to be ourselves.

CAT POEMS

There's a poem in every cat,
      and a cat in every poem.

A Challenge

To a cat, the mouse that runs
is almost as interesting
as the rat that stays.
Both are a challenge.

TASTE THE MEAT,
LICK THE CRUMBS

The cat moves,
every whisker alert
for love, for death,
the countless adventure of
hunting new experiences,
savoring new meanings.
The cat tastes the meat,
it licks the crumbs,
digesting a lifetime
and the promise
       of
       more.

LOST IN WHISKERED DREAMS

With nine lives,
sooner or later,
you'll get grace,
you'll know perfection.
But for the rest of us,
we have one life,
one chance
to get it right.
There's no waiting around,
lost in whiskered dreams,
no hoping someone else will fill our bowl.
We must do it on our own,
hunting in ways that kill us,
prowling through dark alleys,
picking through trash,
looking for that one damn mouse,
the one that gives it all meaning.

THE CAT IS US

The cat is us
as we wish life could be.
The cat is the truth of us,
the whole of us,
perfectly formed,
perfectly mannered
from birth
to go it alone,
to wander far,
yet stay close
to its nature.

For all his miracles,
man cannot say the same.

No Need for Words

I love cats.
I bond with them easily,
far more than people.
They are my friends,
the kind that never judge,
never betray.
We don't have complex conversations,
but we do have deep ones—
the kind shared by long, sleepy blinks,
the pat of a paw,
the pet of a hand.
There's no need for words,
no need for anything but love.

ABOUT THE AUTHOR

Jackson Dean Chase brings you Bold Visions of Dark Places. He is the author of the award-winning poetry collection, *Bukowski's Ghost: Poems for Old Souls in New Bodies*, as well as a growing number of chapbooks, including: *Christmas Eve in the Drunk Tank*, *Be the Magic*, and *Worms Ate Your Face: Horror Poems for Goth and Ghouls*. When not creating poetry, Jackson writes Young Adult fiction and nonfiction self-help books for writers.

Thank you for buying *Crazy Cat Poems for Crazy Cat People!*

If you enjoyed it, **please leave a review**. Even if it's just a few lines, your words make a difference helping my poems reach new readers.

Have a question or suggestion? Just want to say hi?

Jackson loves to connect with his fans.

    Website: JacksonDeanChase.com

    Facebook: Facebook.com/jacksondeanchase

    Twitter: @Jackson_D_Chase

    Tumblr: JacksonDeanChase.tumblr.com

    Email: jackson@jacksondeanchase.com

Want to know when Jackson's next book is coming out?

To receive the latest news on upcoming releases and get **FREE** books, sign up at: **www.JacksonDeanChase.com**. Your email address will never be shared or sold, and you can unsubscribe at any time.

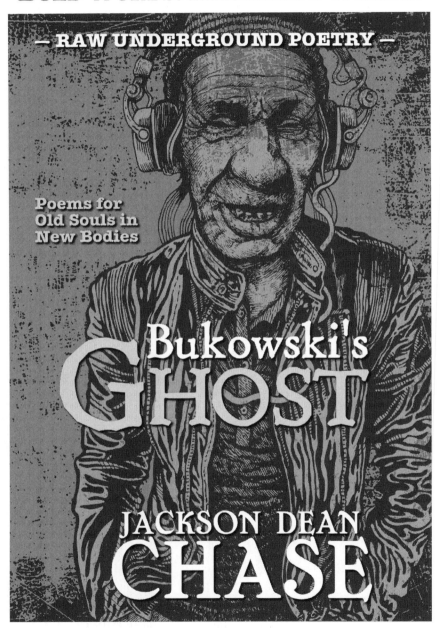

Another Wasted Night

I am drunk on regret, on knowing
   I'll never be good enough.
This diner is old, comforting,
   like my mother's hands.
I slide into a booth and order fries
   wanting to taste love,
   wanting to taste anything
   but what I feel right now.

True Poems

True poems are not safe:
   They must murder some part of you
      while giving birth to another . . .

People love me. People hate me. And I do a little of both. What you are about to read is my personal poetry. Words I bled for, words I own as much as they own me. With them, you can see not just into the deepest part of my soul, but into your own darkness, your own light. You might be surprised what you find.

Life is pain, life is love. It's also short, and I'm tired of wasting mine hiding from the world. I want to share myself. I want to be with you now, in this moment.

And so I am.

— Jackson Dean Chase

www.JacksonDeanChase.com